UNDERSTANDING BIBLE TEACHING

The Christian Vocation

Colin A Grant BSc, BD

Scripture Union

47 Marylebone Lane, London W1 6AX

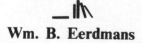

Wm. B. Eerdmans

225 Jefferson Avenue, Grand Rapids, Michigan

© 1974 Scripture Union
First published 1974
First published in this form 1978

All Rights Reserved. No part of this publication may be
reproduced, stored in a retrieval system, or transmitted, in
any form or by any means, electronic, mechanical,
photocopying, recording or otherwise, without the prior
permission of Scripture Union.

ISBN 0 85421 714 2 (Scripture Union)
ISBN 0 8028 1771 8 (Wm. B. Eerdmans)

Printed in Great Britain at the Benham Press
by William Clowes & Sons Limited, Colchester and Beccles

General Introduction

There are many commentaries on the Biblical text and there are many systematic studies of Christian doctrine, but these studies are unique in that they comment on selected passages relating to the major teachings of the Bible. The comments are designed to bring out the doctrinal implications rather than to be a detailed verse by verse exposition, but writers have always attempted to work on the basis of sound exegetical principles. They have also aimed to write with a certain devotional warmth, and to demonstrate the contemporary relevance of the teaching.

These studies were originally designed as a daily Bible reading aid and formed part of Scripture Union's Bible Characters and Doctrines series. They can, of course, still be used in this way but experience has shown that they have a much wider use. They have a continued usefulness as a summary and exposition of Biblical teaching arranged thematically, and will serve as a guide to the major passages relating to a particular doctrine.

Writers have normally based their notes on the RSV text but readers will probably find that most modern versions are equally suitable. Many, too, have found them to be an excellent basis for group Bible study. Here the questions and themes for further study and discussion will prove particularly useful—although many individuals will also find them stimulating and refreshing.

ONE

The Missionary Purposes of God in the Old Testament

1: Boundaries of Blessing

Genesis 12.1–3; 22.15–18

'Why did God choose so small and unknown a tribe as Israel for such special purposes? Why overlook the rest of the world?' are the frequently put questions. God's words to Abram, the father of Israel, make it abundantly clear that there was nothing parochial about the matter at all (12.2 f.; 22.18). God in His wisdom has committed Himself to human instruments in order to convey His blessings to the nations of the world. He has chosen men to reach men, and that was why He chose Abram. He needed a people to reach 'the peoples', and that was why in Abram He chose a nation, the nation of Israel. 'Election is for service. And if God chose Israel, it was not alone that He might reveal Himself to her but that He might claim her for service' writes H. H. Rowley. She was selected, not because of her national grandeur or her numerical strength (Deut. 7.7), but because God has always chosen to reveal His glory through the few (1 Sam. 14.6; Luke 9.1) and the weak (2 Chron. 20.12; 2 Cor. 12.10).

Abram and his descendants were themselves, of course, to rejoice in a personal knowledge of God and an experience of His blessings (cf. 12.2; 22.17). But Abram was being taught that when God gives, He gives in over-flowing measure, so that there would be plenty available for others too! The variant renderings in 12.3 of 'shall . . . be blessed' (AV[KJV]) and 'shall bless themselves' (RSV) depend on the understanding of the use of the Hebrew verb as passive or reflexive; the New Testament application of the phrase (Acts 3.25; Gal. 3.8) would indicate the rightness of the former, though both are very similar in meaning. The phrases 'all the families of the earth' and 'all the nations of the earth' are symbolic of everything else in the Old Testament in relation to mission and foreshadow the great 'alls' of the New Testament (e.g. Matt. 28. 19; 1 Cor. 9. 22).

The principle of 'through *a* people to *all* the peoples' is central in the Biblical understanding of mission. Israel failed in great measure to fulfil her responsibilities in relation to it, and the Church has been very dilatory too. For Christians commitment to God is commitment also to His mission in all the world.

Abram's parish, as well as that of John Wesley, was the world. How big is yours?

2: Consequences of Election

Deuteronomy 10.12–19; 1 Kings 8.33–43

Israel were proud of the fact that they were 'the chosen people of God', but they had to learn that there was a clear 'requirement' (Deut. 10.12) built in to this privilege. The first requirement was a whole-hearted devotion to God in terms of holy reverence, implicit obedience and loving service (Deut. 10.12 f.). Here were the features of that distinctiveness which was meant to identify Israel among the people of the eastern Mediterranean lands and beyond.

Lest, however, such devotion should lead to the cultivation of a secluded form of piety, God emphasized to Israel that their godliness must be accompanied by a concern for others, particularly 'the sojourner' (Deut. 10.19), the non-Israelite who had come to settle down among the people of Israel. Love for the sojourner stems firstly from God's own love for him (Deut. 10.18, cf. Psa. 146.9) and secondly from the fact that because Israel themselves were 'sojourners' in Egypt for 400 years (Deut. 10.19, cf. Gen. 15.13) they should realize only too well the need to understand and care for such people.

Included in the orbit of Solomon's prayer was another type of person, 'the foreigner' (1 Kings 8.41 ff.). This term referred primarily to a non-Israelite living in his own country but which had also 'acquired a religious connotation because of the association of other nations with idolatry' (H. M. Carson). While God's main commands to Israel regarding 'the foreigner' concerned the need for a clear separation from his ungodly ways of life (e.g. Exod. 34.11 ff.), Solomon visualized the occasion when a foreigner with a sincere desire to seek God and attracted by Israel's witness to Him would come to the fellowship of Israel

(42). Such would be an outstanding opportunity for God to reveal His concern for men beyond the borders of the Israelite nation and for Gentiles to be joined with Israel in worshipping the one, true God (43).

The world into which God sends us begins with 'the sojourner', the person living, studying, working, shopping, spending his leisure alongside of us. If we cannot witness effectively to 'the world where it begins' at this point, then it will be somewhat artificial to express interest in 'the foreigner' in 'the world overseas'. The Old Testament teaches us that genuine compassion will include both.

How many people are attracted to you because they have noticed God's power and presence in your life (cf. 1 Kings 8.42)?

3: Conquests of Kingship

Psalm 2

What a great Messianic Psalm this is! After the angry turbulence of the nations in rebellion against God (1–3), we are pointed to God's triumphant vindication of His sovereignty through the resurrection (cf. Acts 13.33) and enthronement (cf. Heb. 1.5, 5.5) of His Son (4–7). Notice that the enthronement of the Son is in special relationship to Mount Zion (6). This latter name was that originally given to the hill on which Jerusalem was built but at times was used to personify the people of God themselves (e.g. Psa. 97.8). This important truth of God's King enthroned for His people is seen in such New Testament verses as Eph. 1.22 and Matt. 28.18 f. where Jesus is declared to be 'head over all things *for the church*', and His supreme authority is the basis of the Church's mandate for world mission.

In the third major section of this psalm, (8–11) we 'overhear' the Father inviting His Son to request universal dominion with a view to exercising universal judgement (8 f.) and the whole of Scripture echoes with the fact that the request has been both made and answered (cf. Matt. 25.31 ff.; Rev. 11.15). Stemming from this declaration of universal sovereignty is an appeal to the kings and rulers of the earth to 'be wise', to cease from their raging and rebellion and turn to God in faith and submission. The Hebrew of vs. 11 and 12 is somewhat uncertain, but the rendering of the

7

RSV is as accurate as any. The concept of 'kissing the feet' as an expression of homage and worship may appear strange to Western ears, but is perfectly acceptable when seen against the oriental background of the Bible.

The appeal to men on the grounds of impending or future judgement is not an uncommon one in the Bible (e.g. Luke 3.7–9; Acts 17.30 f.). Have we today become so uncertain of the truth of divine judgement that we try to avoid the theme altogether? Jesus Christ is both Saviour of those who believe and the sovereign Judge of all men (John 3.16 f.; Acts 17.31). Our presentation of the gospel to the world will only be effective if it is in full accord with both of these truths.

How much do you 'see' Jesus Christ as King of kings and Lord of lords in today's world (cf. 2 Kings 6.17; Heb. 2.9)?

4: Patterns of Righteousness

Isaiah 2.1–4; 11.1–10

These two passages may be interpreted in varying ways. Some view them symbolically, relating them to the historic development of God's Kingdom among men. Others interpret them literally, applying them to a future 'millennial age' on earth. Yet others admit both of these interpretations, viewing the first as a partial and the second as a final fulfilment. A good deal depends on our general approach to Old Testament prophecy. Each must decide from his understanding of the rest of Scripture the interpretation that is the most satisfactory for him.

In the first passage, the exaltation of the Lord, represented by the elevating of His dwelling place high over the lesser peaks of human achievement and pride (cf. 12–16), is a precursor to the 'flowing' of the nations to Him (2) in order that they may hear God's Word and submit themselves to it (3). We note again that the testimony of the Lord to the nations is inextricably linked with His people in 'Zion'. A consequence of this submission of the peoples to God is a new standard of social righteousness, with hatred and warfare being displaced by love and peace in international relationships (4). The horizontal relationship of man with man is directly connected with the vertical relationship of

8

man with God. Put the latter right, and the former is rectified too (cf. Luke **19**.1–10; 1 John **4**.20 f.).

The promised One of David's line, in the second passage, will be equipped for His ministry, not by inherited abilities, but by the endueing of the Spirit. This will give him three pairs of qualities necessary, in turn, for good government ('wisdom and understanding'), effective warfare ('counsel and might') and spiritual leadership ('knowledge and the fear of the Lord') (2). His ministry of judgement among men will be both just and decisive (4 f.), and relationships within the natural order will be transformed through Him (6 f., cf. Rom. **8**. 19–23).

With all the interplay of detail in these two great Isaianic passages, the transforming effect of Messiah's rule in the hearts of men of all nations stands out. When He is present, nothing can be the same again. Because He is God indeed, men and nature yield to the power of His touch.

What are the most urgently needed directions for the social out-workings of the gospel in today's world?

5: Purposes of Grace

Isaiah 19

In this 'oracle', Egypt, Israel's deceitful and undependable Gentile neighbour (Isa. **20**.1 ff.; **30**.1 ff.; **31**.1 ff. etc.), is scheduled for judgement, with its religion (1), unity (2), confidence (3), independence (4), natural resources (5–8) and rural industry (9 f.) feeling the impact of God's power. The whole nation is depicted as morally confused (11–15), and when God uses Israel in judgement against its peoples, they will 'tremble with fear' (16 f.).

Nevertheless, a 'yet more glorious day' is envisaged for Egypt, and how these words must have amazed those who heard them. In spite of Egypt's shady past and the deluge of judgement already predicted, God's purpose for this land will bring blessing not only to the nation but through them to the world. Isaiah sees the day when there will be a community who honour and serve Him within Egypt's borders (18). 'An altar to the Lord', the symbol of true worship, and a 'sacred pillar', a sign of declared allegiance and victory (Gen. **28**.18 ff.; Exod. **24**.4), will represent Egypt's fidelity to God, who in turn, will make their cause His own in times of national emergency (19 f.). God will reveal Himself to Egypt, speaking in order to obtain a response of faith (21 f.) and wounding in order to heal (cf. Deut. 32.39).

That God would actually reveal Himself to Egypt must have been startling enough to Israelite ears. Even more amazing, however, would have been the news of future brotherhood and joint worship between Assyria and Egypt (23) with blessing flowing out to all the world from an Israel–Egypt–Assyria triumvirate.

Nothing could be clearer regarding the inclusion of the Gentiles within the purposes of God. This remains true, whether one views this passage literally, to be fulfilled at the end of time, or symbolically, seeing the conversion of Egypt and Assyria as representing the winning of the Gentiles in the gospel age. The terms 'the work of my hands' and 'my people', used of God's relationship with Israel (cf. Isa. 29.23; 60.21; Lev. 26.12; Ezek. 34.30), are now applied without qualification to Gentile peoples, making them, in Paul's words, 'fellow heirs, members of the same body, and partakers of the promise' (Eph. 3.6).

Is your witness being hindered by an incredulity about the possible conversion of some of your more 'hardened' workmates, neighbours or friends (cf. Acts 9.1–19)?

6: Characteristics of Christ

Isaiah 42.1–13; 49.1–7

These two passages are the first in a series of 'Servant Songs' in Isaiah (the others being found in 50.4–9; 52.13–53.12 and 61.1–4) in which the features of 'he who is to come' (Matt. 11.3) are clearly revealed.

The words 'my servant' are applied elsewhere by Isaiah to Israel as a nation (cf. 41.8 f.; 44.1 f.). The Hebrew mind easily gathered the plural into a personified singular; yet something much more than this is indicated in the Servant Songs. Here is someone who not only fulfilled but far exceeded all that the nation of Israel was meant to be and do.

The ministry of the Servant was firstly to be *unique in character* (42.1; 49.1 f.). The pronoun 'my' spells out an intimacy of relationship; God's purposes were to be clear to Him from birth, and His life was to be energized by God's Spirit (cf. Matt. 3.13-17). Secondly, His ministry was to be *global in extent* (42.1, 4; 49. 1, 6). It was to be concerned with establishing 'justice' among men. This word, in this context, means 'true religion as a rule and law for life in all its relations' (Delitzsch). This ministry is to reach 'the nations', 'coasts and islands', 'peoples far away' and 'earth's farthest bounds' (NEB), and nothing could be more global than that (cf. John 10.16)! In the third place, the ministry of the Servant was to be *exemplary in quality* (42.2 f.; 49.2 f.). He would be no 'ranter', raucously peddling his verbal wares. He would be exquisitely tender among the bruised and flickering spirits of men, not harshly stamping on them as would others, but reaching out in love to reclaim and restore (cf. John 8.1-11). Fourthly, the Servant's life would show a *tenaciousness in purpose* (42.4; 49.4). With a Hebrew play on words, the writer pictures Him as not 'burning out' or being 'bruised away' until His goal is reached. The arrow of His life would hit the centre of the target, despite the apparently meagre reward for His labours (cf. John 1.10-12; 17.4). Finally, the Servant's ministry would be *enlightening in results* (42.6 f.; 49.6). Darkness is a frequently used picture of the spiritual state of both Israel and the Gentile nations, and the Servant would bring the light of the knowledge of God to both (cf. John 8, 12).

Little wonder that the peoples of the earth sing for joy and coastland settlers echo God's praise (42.10-12; cf. Psa. 96.11 f.), and the breadth of the writer's outlook is again featured by the inclusion within his 'choir' of the Bedouin-type desert wanderers of Kedar, one of Israel's adversaries, and the Edomite dwellers of the rocky Sela plateau.

How much does our preoccupation with 'the machinery of mission' (e.g. its magazines, films or personalities) prevent us from being gripped by the glory of the Servant Lord of mission?

7: Dissatisfactions of Idolatry

Jeremiah 16.14-21; Zephaniah 3.8-10

Idolatry is a universal human tragedy. Because of the corruption and rebellion of his sinful heart, man basically refuses to worship and serve the God who made him and instead designs alternative objects for dependence and trust.

Jeremiah reminds Judah that the God who sees all (17) has observed their rebellious idolatry. The idols they adore are no better than carcasses, and as such defile the land (18). An idol is seen as an inheritance of 'sham' (19, NEB). Revered as true objects of worship, they are, in fact 'no gods' (cf. Psa. 96.5, where a Hebrew play on words identifies the 'nations' gods, *elohim*, as nothings, *elilim*, and 1 Cor. 8.4–6, where Paul contrasts 'so-called gods' with the one true God). There is no comparison between what they offer and the security God gives to those who 'from the ends of the earth' turn to Him (19).

A contemporary of Jeremiah, Zephaniah moves from the severe warnings of judgement for Judah and her neighbours, which have occupied him for most of his prophecy, to a vision of God's final judgement of the nations (8). His is the prerogative to 'gather' them for this purpose and the heat of His just reaction against their cumulated sin and rebellion will destroy the earth as well (cf. 2 Pet. 3.10 ff.). Yet, the outlook is not completely bleak. He who judges in righteousness is also He who acts in renewing power in men's hearts (9). The divisive judgement of Babel will be ended (Gen. 11.9) as the nations serve God 'with one accord'. 'Ethiopia' (the 'Cush' of the NEB is the transliteration of the Hebrew), one of the most distant of the nations known to Israel, symbolizes the worship the Gentiles will bring (10). Some scholars have seen a reference here to the regathering of a specifically Jewish dispersion, a common theme in the Old Testament (cf. Jer. 31. 10; Ezek. 11.7, etc.); the NEB with its 'my suppliants of the Dispersion' seems to assume it too. There is, however, no need for such a restricted interpretation.

What different forms does idolatry take among 'the nations' today?

8: Patterns of Discipleship

Jonah 1 and 2

Nineveh, the capital of Israel's last great enemy, Assyria, was the concentrated expression of heathenism and evil to the people of Israel. From this city, the Assyrian kings had vaunted their powers, campaigning for the nation's god, Ashur, and his many consorts, in order to subdue all who would not acknowledge his sovereignty. Against such a city, God commissioned Jonah for mission (1.1). Jonah, in his righteous disgust at the evil parade of the Assyrian capital, was basically unwilling to give any opportunity for God to have mercy on the city (cf. 3.10–4.2); for while God's mandate was indeed a message of denunciation (1.2), Jonah was well acquainted with the forgiving nature of the God he served.

With a mixture of shame and fear, both usually present when man disobeys God, Jonah headed for Tarshish, a trading centre on the coast of Spain and supposedly far away from the uncomfortable and demanding 'presence' of God. But the One who 'brings the wind out of His storehouses' (Psa. 135.7, NEB) and who made the sea and all it contains (cf. Exod. 20.11) exercised His sovereignty in both realms (1.4, 17). Even when God's servants disobey Him, they can never completely evade His all-embracing purposes for them and through the grace of God Jonah was soon being humbled before Him (1.12) and voicing thanksgiving to His Name (2.9).

The relationship of Christian disobedience to the fulfilling of the perfect will of God on earth is bound up in mystery. Centuries passed in the history of Christendom with the gospel being withheld from the world because of the denial of it by those who should have been sharing it. Even after the Reformation, the Church only slowly roused itself to take the gospel to all peoples and today much still remains to be done despite all that has been accomplished since William Carey arrived in India in 1793. Yet from our studies today and tomorrow, it will become quite clear that God in His wisdom, patience and grace, is able to gather up our human imperfection and still cause His goals to be attained and the ends of the earth to hear of His glory.

In relation to our disobedience in the task of mission, is this another case where 'the goodness of God' should lead us 'to repentance' (cf. Rom. 2.4)?

9: Principles of Mercy
Jonah 3 and 4

God spoke persistently and patiently 'the second time'. The servant of God had been chastened, but while his outward actions

13

indicated obedience, his reactions afterwards (e.g. **4.1 ff.**) continued to show a grudging spirit. In Nineveh, the response was dramatic (**3.5 ff.**). God exercised His pardon (cf. Exod. **33.19**; Psa. **86.5**) and withheld His judgement (**3.10**). The use of the word 'repented' in **3.10** in relation to God implies, not, of course, a regret for previous or intended actions, but a sovereign change in His dealings with men in just accord with a new response and obedience on their part and in perfect harmony with His own nature.

To Jonah, the 'worst' had happened! Blatant evil had received mercy not judgement and it seemed as though God was allowing past evil to go unpunished. Jonah's failing was 'the sin of pretending to be more careful of God's glory and more qualified to advance it than God Himself' (Hugh Martin), and it led him to offer a confused prayer (**4.2 f.**) and to slink away under a cloud of self-embitterment (**4.5**). It may seem amazing to us that the repentance and pardon of ungodly men could lead to such a reaction, yet Jonah's aggrieved attitude was but a logical consequence of his basic unwillingness to obey God. Moreover, it was a reflection of the prevailing attitude within Israel as a whole at that time.

To show Jonah something of the religious exclusiveness that had been binding and blinding him, God spoke finally through an acted parable. Jonah's feelings at the withering of the gourd that had given him such valuable, if brief, protection were strong (**4.9 f.**). If Jonah could be capable of such deep emotion towards a mere plant that he had neither planted nor nourished, could not he begin to understand how greatly God Himself must care over an urban concentration of thousands of men and women whom He had created and who, in their ignorance, were in so much need of His pardon and true knowledge of Himself?

*Tokyo (nearly 12 million), London (7½ million), Moscow (nearly 7¼ million), Sao Paulo (nearly 7½ million). What is your attitude towards the people of such cities? (cf. Luke **13**.34).*

Questions and themes for study and discussion on Studies 1-9

1. 'Election has no goal in itself, but only the Kingdom of God' (C. Vriezen). How far does this summarize the Old Testament teaching on God's choice of Israel?

2. What do the final three 'Servant Songs' (see Study 6) teach on Christ's world-wide ministry?
3. What are the basic causes for disobedience among present-day Christians in their task of world-wide witness?

TWO

Mission and the Son of God

10: Focus of the Prophets

Luke 4.16–30

This incident could be quite separate from that recorded in Matt. 13.53–58 and Mark 6.1–6, or Luke might have brought it ahead of its exact chronological placing because of its excellent symbolic introduction to the ministry of Jesus that he was to tell. In reading verses from the prophets, our Lord responds to the usual invitation given to a travelling rabbi (cf. Acts 13.15 ff.) after the prescribed portion from the law had been read by one of the resident teachers of the synagogue. Jesus reads from Isa. 61.1–4 (probably the fifth of the 'Servant Songs'), the minor modifications we notice in the Gospel account being the result of Luke's dependence on the Septuagint and the incorporation by our Lord of an additional phrase, reflecting Isa. 58.6, which further enlarges on the ministry of 'The Servant' in liberating the oppressed among men. He who could say of the Scriptures 'Their testimony points to me' (John 5.39, NEB, cf. 1 Pet. 1.10–12) leaves His hearers in no doubt as to the One about whom Isaiah was writing (21)! He would be the instrument both for effecting as well as for proclaiming the long awaited New Age when God would grant deliverance to men in a way hitherto unparalleled in human history.

Anticipating the eventual rejection by His hearers of both Himself and His claim, He shows that when faced with similar rejection and unbelief from Israel, both Elijah and Elisha were used in blessing to Gentiles (24–27, cf. 1 Kings 17.8–16; 2 Kings 5.1–14).

No wonder the sensitive Jewish audience was 'infuriated' (28, NEB) and took measures to kill Him (29 f.)! In the succeeding months and years, it was to be seen that the global bounds of the Old Testament Scriptures were the very categories that would characterize His own ministry and that of His Church. The

16

responsibility for making known the glory of God in the world, a task in which Israel had so tragically failed, would be uniquely fulfilled in Him; whatever the consequences, He would not be party to the false parochialism of His fellow-countrymen.

Are we too institutionalized and 'respectable' to mix sufficiently with people where they are so that Christ can 'announce good news' and 'set captives free' through us today?

11:·Seeker of the Lost

Luke 15

The immediate occasion for much of our Lord's teaching was the need to minister to those who misunderstood and criticized Him. The set of three parables we study today comes within this grouping (cf. 1 f.). To the Jew, 'a sinner' was both one who lived an openly immoral life and one who followed a dishonourable calling (see *The Parables of Jesus* by Joachim Jeremias). The eagerness of such people to hear Jesus stood out in stark contrast to the offended pride of the Pharisees. As we see our Lord welcoming 'sinners', we realize that His attitude 'is no mere humanitarian enthusiasm ... but the manifestation of the will and purpose of God' (T. W. Manson).

The first two parables (4–7; 8–10) with their ancillary lessons of persistent and patient seeking for that which is lost, point us primarily to 'the redemptive joy of God'. It is this joy in which the Pharisees ought to have been sharing rather than being soured through their proud self-righteousness. Pharisees were, of course, prepared to welcome the repentant sinner if the latter would come to them. Jesus showed them that the love of God is of a different quality altogether.

In our traditional focus on 'the Prodigal Son' of the third parable (11–32), we have tended to overlook that the story is more properly geared to teach us primarily about 'The Loving Father'. His watching, waiting love surges forward in a run, an embrace and a royal welcome when the repentant son of the family returns. Here was no cool and calculated response, such as could be expected from the Pharisees; and there was certainly no semblance of that grudging 'stand-offishness' shown by the second son of the family, in whom the Pharisees were meant to

17

detect their own image. The hardness of their own hearts is crushingly demonstrated in the parable's depiction of the Father being ready to 'go out' *to his eldest son also* in order to reason with him regarding his attitude (28).

When love is not prepared to spend itself in seeking the lost of its neighbourhood, whatever may be the cost in time, personal convenience and public esteem, and when love becomes so formalized that the repentant sinner is just another notch on a 'church growth' report, then that 'love' is 'good for nothing' and becomes mere noise (Matt. 5.13; 1 Cor. 13.1).

12: Saviour of the World

John 4.1–42

During His direct journey from Jerusalem to Galilee (3 f.), Jesus took the opportunity of His meeting with the Samaritan woman (cf. *New Bible Dictionary* on 'Samaritans') to minister to her need. In so doing, He set aside the traditional Jewish prejudices of sex and race in such a situation, and foreshadowed the bringing of the gospel to the people of that land by the early Christians (cf. Acts 8.1) and by Philip in particular (cf. Acts 8.5 ff.). After His offer to her of 'living water' (7–15), the woman recognized something of our Lord's spiritual stature through His exposure of her life (16–18). She hastened to turn the conversation away from herself to the question of the respective merits of Mount Gerizim, the Samaritan centre of devotion, and Jerusalem as suitable locations for the worship of God (20). The reply of Jesus states the basic principle that true worship is not a question of correct geography but of correct spiritual understanding (21–23). The dawning of God's New Age would indeed come from preparatory revelation possessed by the Jews, and not from the Samaritan's partial and confused patterns (22); but because the true God is 'spirit' (not 'a spirit' as in AV [KJV]), those who worship Him must possess corresponding qualities of heart (24). Such, whether they be in Borneo, Brazil, Britain or Burundi, will, if the focus of their faith is Jesus Christ, 'the truth', be accepted (cf. John 14.6; Mal. 1.11; Acts 10.35). Such will never be cast out (cf. John 6.37).

As a result of the woman's eager testimony (28 ff.), the first fruits of the spiritual harvest among the Samaritan nation were gathered (39, 41). The testimony of these new believers was to One whose blessings of salvation were not for the Jews only but for them also, representatives as they were of 'the world' (42).

Jesus used such a time of spiritual reaping to urge on His disciples the need to take advantage of every immediate opportunity to do God's will among men and not to remain inactive in the mistaken belief that 'the time is not yet ripe' (35 f.). He Himself had just given them an unforgettable example of how to minister 'in season and out of season' (2 Tim. 4.2).

Is your church guilty of awaiting 'a suitable season' to minister to its neighbourhood?

13: Friend of the Needy

Matthew 15.21–28

To the Jew, the Phoenician coastal towns of Tyre and Sidon (21) 'were not places where Messianic works were destined to be performed' (R.V.G. Tasker, cf. 11.21). Yet Jesus once more takes the opportunity to minister to another Gentile woman whose people followed a popular religious blend of polytheism and fertility cults. 'In the background was her religion, in the foreground was her need,' writes G. Campbell Morgan. Her lips express the cry of a mother's aching heart (22) to the visiting 'Son of David', of whose fame she had no doubt heard (cf. 4.24).

Our Lord's initial reluctance to help her (23, 26) was an expression of His prior sense of purpose to those who, of all peoples, should have been prepared for His coming (cf. 10.5 f.; Rom. 15.8 f.). For this reason, He was unwilling to become caught up during His earthly life in a large scale mission among Gentile people. His statement of intent (24), however, did but evoke an open-hearted plea, urgent in its simplicity (25, cf. 14.30). Our Lord's reply (26) 'was not a simple monosyllabic negative . . . but an argument inviting further discussion' (A. B. Bruce), with the word used in vs. 26 f. for dog *kunarion* being the diminutive form meaning the household dog rather than the savage 'pariah' of the streets. The woman assents to the principle (27) and with a blend of humility, humour, faith and spiritual insight presses her plea.

Once before, Jesus had occasion to marvel at a Gentile's great faith and on that occasion too He had healed at a distance (28; 8.5–13). Against the hostility of Jewish officialdom, such 'faith active in love' (Gal. 5.6, NEB) must have been refreshing indeed! God's Spirit moves in what are often, to our eyes, the most unexpected of places and the most surprising of people. Yet, far from being taken unawares, we should be serving and praying in anticipation of just this (cf. Isa. 65.1).

Genuine faith wherever it appears is always 'given' faith (cf. Acts 14.27; Eph. 2.8).

14: Shepherd of the Sheep
John 10.11–16; 11.47–53

Jesus, the Good Shepherd, proves the genuineness of His credentials not only by fidelity to His flock, even to the sacrifice of His own life on their behalf (10.11–15), but by His compelling purpose to gather those 'sheep' still outside of His fold (10.16). The AV (KJV), by too much dependence on the Vulgate, disguises the two separate Greek words used in v. 16 for 'fold' (*aulē*) and 'flock' (*poimnē*), cf. RSV and NEB; 'the sheep not of this fold are non-Jewish Christians. Only when all that are Christ's, in whatever fold they may be found, have responded to the gospel will the ideal of one flock under one shepherd be a reality' (R. V. G. Tasker). The 'must' of Christ impelled Him not only to seek and save the lost during His earthly years (cf. Luke 19.10) but to offer His life in a substitutionary death, planned so cruelly by the unscrupulous political manoeuvrings of Caiaphas (11.50) and yet centred so surely in the sovereign purposes of God (10.17 f.; Acts 2.23). This death would form the basis for the world-wide 'gathering' that was to follow, in which Jew and Gentile alike would find personal relationship with God (11.52, cf. 1.12; Gal. 3.26 ff.).

The misguided conservatism of the Jewish leaders would have denied that God had a redeeming purpose for any fold outside that of Judaism. Even some in the Early Church at first insisted that a Gentile should be 'in Israel' as well as 'in Christ' (cf. Acts 15.5; Gal. 2.4 ff.). No wonder the Spirit of Truth had to shatter such views (cf. Acts 15.19 ff.; Gal. 3.1 ff.)! In view of the Church today having lost so much of that dynamic mobility for 'seeking' and 'gathering' that should characterize its life, one of its paramount needs is a similar 'shattering' experience from the Holy Spirit.

If you would have Jesus as the Good Shepherd to lead you 'beside still waters' (Psa. 23.2), you must have Him also as the One who, through you, 'must bring' the lost to Himself (10.16), whatever the cost (cf. 15.18 ff.).

15: Victor of the Cross

John 12.20–36

'The world has gone after Him,' scoffed the Pharisees (19), but the universal appeal of Jesus was illustrated far more effectively than they actually desired through the earnest enquiry of the Greek proselytes in Jerusalem for the Passover Feast (20 f.)! Our Lord was aware that 'His hour' (23, 27, cf. 2.4; 7.30, etc.) was upon Him, and as part of 'the glory' of it, He saw 'the rich harvest' (24, NEB) that would follow His being 'sown in the ground' through death. The coming of the Greeks was a first fruits of that greater turning to Him from the Gentile world which was the hope of all Scripture and of which He had already spoken (cf. 10.16).

Jesus was deeply conscious of all that would be involved in the Cross. He contemplated the hypothetical alternative of requesting His Father to save Him from (Gk. *ek* out of) it all (27), yet He refused it immediately with a firm 'No' (cf. Matt. 26.39). The whole course of His life lay in the direction of Calvary, and He had repeatedly rejected the Evil One's subtle overtures to follow an easier but defeatist path (Matt. 4.8 f.; 16.22 f.). These initial victories were portents of that greater victory over Satan which would be gained at the Cross itself when he, 'the ruler of this world' would be 'ejected from his dominion' (Marcus Dods) and deprived of his power to hold the hearts and wills of men in thraldom (31, cf. 16.11). The decisive nature of Christ's death at the Cross interpreted as a victory over the powers of evil is continued throughout the New Testament and forms the basis for our Lord's right and power to 'draw all men' to Himself (32, cf. 6.44 where the same verb *helkō* is used).

How are we to interpret the 'all' in this verse? If it means 'all

21

without exception', then we are faced either with a universalistic interpretation whereby 'all will eventually be saved', a line of teaching contrary to Scripture as a whole (cf. Matt. 25.46; John 3.36; Rev. 20.11 ff.), or with the need to read it with the sense of drawing to salvation *and* to judgement, an idea which 'cannot be excluded in view of v. 31' (Donald Guthrie). It would seem better, however, to see 'all' as meaning 'all without distinction', men from every nation, whether they be Jew or Gentile, African or European, Buddhist or Moslem, educated or illiterate, rich or poor. This reflects not only the thought of several other passages in John's Gospel (e.g. 4.39 ff.; 10.11 ff.) but also the trend of Scriptural teaching as a whole (Acts 10.34; Rom. 3.21 ff.; Rev. 5.9, etc.).

How much time do you give each week to reading or hearing about 'the drawing power of Christ' among the peoples of the world?

Questions and themes for study and discussion on Studies 10-15

1. 'It is not enough to be told that God loves; the reality of love lies in a region other than that of words' (James Denney). How did this apply to the ministry of our Lord?
2. Among the varieties of religious experience in the world, what are the places where true spiritual need is personally felt?
3. Where is the victory of the Cross to be seen in today's world?

THREE

Mission and the Holy Spirit

16: Empowering for Mission

John 15.22–16.11; 20.19–23

The word 'Comforter' (15.26, AV [KJV]), used to translate the Greek word *paraklētos*, can be traced back to Wycliff, when the word then denoted the giving of strength and courage (cf. Latin *fortis* meaning 'brave'). 400 years have passed and the verb 'to comfort' has mellowed with the years! Jesus spoke to His disciples primarily of an Enabler, an empowering Companion (cf. Eph. 3.16). He would also be the 'Spirit of truth' (15.26) whose ministry of witness to Christ would be closely linked with the disciples' own witness to their Master (15.27). 'The double witness in the world nevertheless would be one witness . . . the witness of the Spirit and the witness of the Church' (Leon Morris). The Spirit witnesses because He is 'the Spirit of Christ' (Rom. 8.9; 1 Pet. 1.11), glorifying Christ (16.14). The disciples witness because their eyes have seen and their hands have touched (1 John 1.1 ff.), and they are thus inescapably and joyously committed.

All true power in mission is to be found in the working of the Spirit in the hearts of men (16.8). In respect of any awareness of truth, 'whatever conscience the world might display is His work' (Donald Guthrie). Through Him, men will realize the tragedy of rejecting Jesus for self-centred independency (16.9); they will acknowledge the genuineness and rightness of all that Jesus claimed to be because of His triumphant vindication from this earthly scene (16.10), and they will tremble with guilt as they see the cause of evil, to which they have given allegiance, humbled and broken through Christ's victory (16.11). When we begin to appropriate for ourselves the ability to bring about such conviction in men through self-devised means, we are immediately launched on something other than Christian mission. Let personal and mass evangelists beware!

Christ had thus spoken of 'the coming One'; now He appoints His disciples for service in the Spirit's power (20.21 f.). In our Lord's use of two different words to mean 'send' in v. 21, Jesus is in fact saying: 'As the Father has commissioned me by delegating to me His authority, so I now despatch you under that same authority.' And to knit the disciples' mission with the promised Holy Spirit, He 'blows' or breathes on them probably in symbolic anticipation of the day when the Spirit would truly 'blow' on them (cf. Acts 2.2 ff.) and they would fully 'receive' Him (cf. Acts 2.38; 10.47). Such empowering is necessary if God's Word is to be convincingly declared to men regarding their sins (cf. 20.23). The Church can but declare what God has already done (cf. Mark 2.7; 1 John 1.9), and while human knowledge can never be omniscient, yet the Christian can confidently declare to the one who truly repents and believes: 'Your sins have been forgiven for His sake' (1 John 2.12, NEB).

How much of the Spirit's 'convicting' work have you seen among your friends in recent days?

17: Categories of Salvation

Luke 24.44–53

The average Jew read about the Messiah in his Old Testament with his eyes open but his mind closed. 'It cannot be that the Messiah will suffer and die; when He comes, it will be as an all-triumphant King!' he wistfully trusted. So a task of 'thoroughly opening up' (the literal meaning of the Greek verb *dianoigō*) was needed (45) for those 'startled and frightened' disciples (37). Jesus showed that not only His suffering, death and resurrection (46) but also the proclaiming of salvation world-wide were foreshadowed in the pages of the sacred book. 'The picture, blurred, indistinct, out of focus, came sharply into focus and they saw the whole thing not in detail but in sequence' (Campbell Morgan).

Never would such tidings as this sound on men's ears! Here were spiritual categories after which men had groped and grasped from the earliest dawn of time and have similarly sought to the present day. The message is centred in two truths. The first is repentance, *metanoia*, that turning from self to God as a result of a humbling awareness of having offended and rebelled against

Him in thought, word and deed. It is a recurrent theme in the Old Testament as God called His people to turn to Him from their waywardness (Isa. 55.7; Jer. 3.12 f, etc.). The need for men to repent was prominent in the message of Jesus (Matt. 4.17, etc.) and in that of the Early Church too (Acts 2.38, etc.). The second category of God's saving message is forgiveness of sins, *aphesis hamartiōn*, that act of God whereby He ceases to reckon a man's misdeeds against him and accounts him guiltless before His bar of justice. Again, it emerges prominently in the Old Testament (Psa. 103.3; Dan. 9.9, etc.), in the teaching of Jesus (Matt. 6.12, etc.) and in the witness of the first Christians (Acts 5.31, etc.). In the saving purposes of God, repentance in fact 'brings' forgiveness (47), and these two are only to be found 'in Christ's Name'. It is for this reason that the gospel stands unique by comparison with the world's secular ideologies and religious teachings.

The proclamation of these tidings had to begin at Jerusalem (47) because it was the historical and symbolical centre of God's dealings with His people and thus, in the sovereign purposes of God, the place where they would be 'invested' (A. B. Bruce) with the needful empowering for their task (49). The Father had promised the Spirit through the prophets (cf. Isa. 44.3; Joel 2.28–32). Through His Son (cf. John 7.38 f.) He had now announced His immediate advent (cf. John 14.16, 26. The Greek verb *exapostellō*, I send forth, v, 49, is in the present tense indicating an imminent future action). The disciples' obedience (52) was to be duly rewarded (cf. Acts 5.32).

Is there any salvation for sincere followers of non-Christian religions apart from a conscious experience of repentance and forgiveness 'in His Name' (47)?

18: Enduement for Service

Acts 1.1–11

Jesus lived and taught in the Holy Spirit's power (2, cf. Luke 4.1, 14). Through the same Spirit He both offered up His life in death (Heb. 9.14) and was openly vindicated as the Son of God through resurrection (Rom. 1.4; 1 Tim. 3.16). His promise to the disciples (4) was thus in full accord with the pattern of His own ministry.

John the Baptist had already contrasted his own baptizing in water with the forthcoming baptism in the Holy Spirit to be effected by Jesus (Mark 1.8; Luke 3.16). Our Lord restates the contrast with His own unique authority and at a new vantage point in time, full of immediate expectation (5, 'within the next few days' NEB). The verb 'to baptize' means, when used literally, 'to wash by dipping or immersing' or when used figuratively 'to overwhelm, to plunge into a new realm of experience'. It was in this latter figurative sense that Jesus used the word in relation to the disciples' impending encounter with the Holy Spirit, in the same way that He used the verb 'to clothe' in Luke 24.49. The terminology of 'baptism' was especially significant in view of the later reference to the Spirit being 'poured out' (2.17, 18, 33; 10.45); the disciples were to be submerged in the Spirit's tidal flow as the New Age was inaugurated. We must be aware of the danger of allowing these and other figurative expressions found in the New Testament relating to the work of the Holy Spirit in the believer's life to harden into 'technical terms', so that a Christian's spiritual standing is measured by how many of them apply to him.

The 'coming upon' them of the Spirit (note the further graphic phrase) would mean power (Gk. *dunamis*, meaning 'ability and strength to perform' as differentiated from *exousia* (7) meaning 'liberty and authority to exercise power', Abbot-Smith). This power would be the motivation for the ministry of witness to which they had been called (8, cf. John 15.27).

Only the Spirit can enable the Church to reach the geographical limits of its task; for not only Jerusalem and its immediate environs would need to hear the good news, but also the whole province of Judea, the neighbouring northern 'half-caste' territory of Samaria and then 'lands without limit' (8).

We can grieve and quench the Holy Spirit (Eph. 4.30; 1 Thess. 5.19) in mission as well as in other aspects of Christian living.

19: Experience of Promise

Acts 2

'At Pentecost, the Holy Spirit empowered a little band of insignificant, ignorant and feeble but believing men and women to undertake the stupendous task of conquering the world for

Christ, their Lord' (R. B. Kuiper). Pentecost (1, meaning 'the fiftieth') fell 50 days after the presentation of the wave sheaf at Passover (cf. Lev. 23.15–21; Deut. 16.9–12). It was one of the three great Jewish festivals to which every Jew, resident within 20 miles of Jerusalem, was bound to come. According to Edersheim, it probably attracted more visitors from a distance than even the Passover itself.

The supernatural and external signs of 'driving wind' and 'flames of fire' (2 f., NEB) were those frequently linked with the power and presence of God (cf. Psa. 104.4; Exod. 19.18). They symbolized an inward experience, the 'filling' of the disciples with the Holy Spirit. That which was promised (1.5, cf. John 15.26) came to pass. We should understand this yet further figurative verb 'to fill' not in the static sense of 'to top-up an empty vessel' but in the dynamic sense of 'to take possession of' or 'control' (cf. 3.10; 5.3, 17; 19.29).

As the Holy Spirit began to fulfil His ministry of interpreting spiritual truth through the disciples (cf. John 15.26), the international crowd, gathered in Jerusalem (9 ff.), began to hear 'the great things God has done' (11, NEB). This came firstly through a miraculously given communication in their own individual dialects (8), and then in straightforward *koinē* Greek or Aramaic (14 ff.; it is not certain which language Peter used here.)

The main purpose of the pouring out of the Spirit (cf. 17 ff.; Joel 2.28–32) was to inaugurate an era when men could call on the name of the Lord and be saved (21). Peter's own clear and illumined presentation of the gospel (22 ff.) was yet a further illustration of this same Spirit of truth at work (John 16.13 f.), for Peter could never have grasped such truths about the Old Testament or his Lord on his own (cf. Matt. 16.17)!

The availability of the Holy Spirit to the obedient and believing is proclaimed by the disciples in their turn to the enquiring crowds (38), and thus it has been passed on in successive ages to people 'far away' (39, NEB).

When did you last 'pass on' the offer?

20: Crossing of Boundaries

Acts 8

The unleashing of persecution against the early believers (1) only served to widen the extent of their witness (4) and Philip moves into Samaritan territory to make Christ known there to mighty effect (5 ff., cf. John 4.4 ff.). Unless we are to accuse Philip of preaching a truncated gospel, which would not appear evident from vs. 5, 35, 40, and to assume the response of the Samaritans to have been spurious, which would not seem to be the natural interpretation of vs. 6, 8, 14, those baptized were truly born again of God's Spirit (cf. John 3.5), had received the Spirit (cf. Gal. 3.2) and were thus indwelt by Him (cf. Rom. 8.9–11; 1 Cor. 3.16). We must thus interpret the verb 'receive' in vs. 17, 19 in terms of the parallel and further figurative verb 'fall on' in v. 16, the latter being used on other occasions when the 'reception' of the Spirit was accompanied by speaking in tongues and similar manifestations (cf. 10.44, 46; 11.15, cf. 19.6 where another pictorial verb 'came upon' is used). 'In the case of the Samaritans no such signs from heaven had followed their baptism, and the Apostles prayed for a conspicuous divine sanction on the reception of the new converts' (A. B. Bruce). It is logical to conclude that what Simon 'saw' (18) and what he thought he could reproduce himself (19) was 'a Samaritan Pentecost', and the laying on of hands (17) was the outward expression of that inner bond of spiritual unity (cf. Eph. 4.3) which Jerusalem and Samaritan believers now enjoyed through their common faith in Christ.

The Spirit of God then directed Philip to minister in a much more individualized situation (26, cf. v. 29). The Ethiopian court official's visit to Jerusalem was prompted by his desire to worship God (27) in contrast to the primitive cultic deities venerated by his fellow-countrymen. 'His conversion (36 ff.) marks a further advance towards the evangelization of the Gentiles' (F. F. Bruce). The joy with which he continued on his way was surely as much a product of the Spirit's working (Gal. 5.22) as were Philip's new directives for service (39, cf. 1 Kings 18.12; 2 Kings 2.16).

How sensitive are you to the promptings of the Spirit for mission in your life (29) and how eager are you to obey (30)?

28

21: Fulfilling of Prophecy

Acts 10

The great moment had come! Peter had already shared in the taking of the gospel to semi-Gentiles (8.14 ff.). Now God was to use him to make the major break-through to the wholly Gentile world. As with other passages of Scripture, while the Spirit is only specifically mentioned on selected occasions (19 f., 38, 44 f., 47) the evidence of His activity is to be seen throughout the narrative, which because of its importance is recorded in the next chapter when recounted by Peter himself (11.1–18).

Despite the godliness of Cornelius and his household (2), he was still traditionally regarded as 'unclean' by such as Peter, for in Jewish eyes, Gentile carelessness with food made social intercourse with them out of the question. God showed Peter (9 ff.) that the areas where He is at work must never be treated with disdain (15) and such an area was this Gentile household (22). With his spiritual understanding clearing at every move (21, 23, 25), Peter confessed how the Spirit of God was changing his traditional prejudices (28). In response to Cornelius' invitation (33) he pointed his hearers to Christ and His power to forgive 'everyone who believes in Him' (43). This inclusive 'everyone' was a consequence of Peter's recognition that God has no favourites (34) and that He is ready to accept the sincere seekings of any person by bringing to them, through His messengers, the news of salvation. We note that Cornelius was not saved on the grounds of his religious sincerity (2, 35) but by his personal trust in Christ (47, cf. 11.17 f.). It is mistaken to conclude from this passage, therefore, that 'religious sincerity' is sufficient to save.

This time, the Holy Spirit 'fell' (44, cf. 8.16) and was 'poured out' (45, cf. 2.17 f., 33) before those who had received Him had been baptized in water (47 f.). 'No routine procedure would have availed for so unprecedented a situation as the acceptance of the gospel by Gentiles; an unmediated act of God was required' writes F. F. Bruce. The unfolding purposes of God in the Old Testament had broken forth in wonder and grace; Jew and Gentile had become 'fellow citizens ... of the household of God', 'members of the same body', 'all one in Christ Jesus' (Eph. 2.19; 3.6; Gal. 3.28). Peter was convinced that God's dealings with both were now without distinction (cf. 11.15, 17 f.) and from the

29

ruins of Jewish traditionalism there was rising the new building of the Church of Jesus Christ.

Can you see any 'traditional structures' in missionary activity today that need renewing by the Holy Spirit?

22: Establishing of Principles

Romans 15.7–21

Paul delights to present Christ as the inaugurator of God's blessings to both Jew and Gentile (8 f.) and draws from the rich veins of the Law, the Prophets and the Writings (the 3 great divisions of the Old Testament) to illustrate the Gentile inheritance in particular (9–12). Isaiah's note of 'hope' (12, cf. Isa. **11.**10) makes a suitable launching pad for him to glorify the God who through His Spirit can make the believer 'overflow with hope' (13, NEB) in the surging confidence that what God has promised will assuredly come true (cf. **5.**4; **15.**4; Col. **1.**27).

Turning to his personal pattern of service 'to the Gentiles' (16), he uses Jewish sacerdotal terminology to describe himself as a priest (Gk. *leitourgos*), his ministry as 'priestly service' (Gk. *hierourgōn*) and the Gentiles as the priestly offering (Gk. *prosphora*) that he presents (16). Perhaps having in mind Jewish believers who might quibble at the correctness of such an 'unclean' offering, Paul declares it 'acceptable' by the operations of the Holy Spirit. Through that Spirit men's hearts are cleansed by faith (cf. Acts **15.**8 f.) and in Him 'the true circumcision', comprising both Jew and Gentile, worship God and find joy in Jesus Christ (Phil. **3.**3).

Despite the high privilege of being called to minister in such a 'priestly service' Paul's only glory continues to be in Christ. His finished work at Calvary (Gal. **6.**14) and continuing work through His servants (18) in the power of the Spirit (19) dominate Paul's heart and mind. Only endued with the Spirit's power could he have demonstrated the divine origin of the gospel through miraculous signs (cf. Acts **19.**11) and preached its truth in every major area of the Roman provinces bordering the Eastern Mediterranean (19 f.). Truly, 'the Holy Spirit is a missionary Spirit creating in God's servants an internal necessity to preach the gospel' (Roland Allen).

'Activity world-wide in its direction and intention . . . is inevitable for us unless we are ready to deny the Holy Spirit of Christ' (*Roland Allen*).

Questions and themes for study and discussion on Studies 16-22

1. 'It is in the revelation of the Holy Spirit as a missionary Spirit that the Acts stands alone in the New Testament.' How far is Roland Allen justified in this statement?
2. How can Christians hinder the Spirit's ministry in world missions today?
3. In what ways can the 'figurative' verbs relating to the Holy Spirit's coming to the Early Church be applied to the Church today?

FOUR

Mission and the Church

23: Men Needed

Luke 9.1–6; 10.1–20

To keep company with Christ involves personal commitment to His purposes. For the twelve disciples, this meant being available for mission. Notice the verbal sequence: 'He called the twelve (1) ... He gave them power (1) ... He sent them out (2)' (cf. Mark 3.14 f.). This embodies a spiritual succession that is apparent throughout Scripture, from God's dealings with Moses (Exod. 3.4, 10 f.) and the prophets (Jer. 1.5–9) to His commissioning of the Early Church (Luke 24.48 f.) and of Paul (Acts 26.16 ff.). The verb *apostellō* translated 'to send' (2) is the root from which the word 'apostle' is derived and basically means 'to send out with instructions to act on the authority of the sender and in his name'. It was in this capacity, then, that the twelve moved out among the towns and villages of Trans-Jordania (6).

The 'heralding' for which they had been appointed was a triumphant announcement that God's kingly rule had begun on earth (2), and this was to be demonstrated not only in word but also in the practical overthrow of Satan's power over men (1, 6, cf. 10.17). If the twelve were sent primarily to minister in this way among the Jews (cf. Matt. 10.5 f. the total probably symbolizing the number of the tribes of Israel), the commissioning of the seventy (10.1, or 'seventy-two' as indicated by a good number of Greek mss. cf. NEB and TEV) could well have had a wider ministry in view (the number is reminiscent of the total of the Gentile nations in Gen. 10 or of the eldership of Israel [Exod. 24.1]). Yet, encouraging as were these wider circles of ministry, they could only touch part of the need, and in the light of the immensity of the task before them, Jesus again urges His disciples to prayer (cf. Matt. 9.37 f., John 4.35), making 'the seventy' the first part of the answer (10.3)!

32

With what readiness to become personally involved do you sing the words: 'Send forth the Gospel, let it run southwards and northwards, east and west'?

24: Men Transformed

Matthew 16.13–28

The conviction to which Peter came concerning the person of Christ (16) was both forthright and divinely inspired (17, cf. 1 Cor. 12.3), and the expressing of it led to our Lord enunciating a major truth regarding His redeeming purposes among men. The confession of Himself as Christ and Son of God (16) or, alternatively, the actual person confessing this truth (both are possible interpretations of v. 18) would be the material upon which He would build the spiritual edifice He called 'His Church'.

The word *ekklesia*, translated 'church', literally means 'that which is called out', and was a word widely used in our Lord's day. In the Graeco-Roman world, it had come to describe any local assembly of Roman citizens, whether democratically convened for legislative purposes or gathered for more informal purposes. In the Greek version of the Old Testament, it is used over seventy times to denote an assembly of the people of Israel summoned to hear what God had to say to them (cf. Deut. 18.16). The suitability of such a word to denote the new community that Jesus would be bringing into being through the gospel is clearly evident, and it became one of the great words of the New Testament. It denoted both the local fellowship of believers (e.g. 1 Cor. 1.2; 1 Thess. 1.1), as well as that wider, all-inclusive fellowship of which the individual fellowship was a local expression (e.g. Acts 20.28; 1 Cor. 10.32). God's salvation is thus not only to be experienced personally but corporately as well, as believers are joined in fellowship together.

In the Acts, we must therefore see those who responded to the gospel in such places as Jerusalem, Antioch and the cities of Galatia in terms of Christ building His Church. Similarly, we note how closely Paul's ministry was bound up with the planting and nourishing of local churches in every place he visited. All true mission today should have the same end in view.

Because the Church of Jesus Christ is made up of those in whose lives the power of Satan has been overthrown (cf. the previous

33

study; also Acts **26**.18; Col. **1**.13), it will never be overpowered by the forces of death (18, NEB). In its outward expression on earth, it may be marred by human deficiencies (e.g. Acts **5**.1–11), suffer setbacks from its enemies (e.g. Acts **12**.1–4) and, as in the case of North Africa in the 7th and China in the 20th centuries, be almost obliterated for a time in certain geographical areas. Yet, because the Church belongs to Christ, the direction and culmination of God's purposes through it are sure (cf. Eph. **5**.22 ff.; Rev. **5**.9 f.).

How far have you realized the personal implications of believing in 'one holy, catholic (*i.e. universal*) and apostolic church' (Nicene Creed)?

25: Men Invited

Matthew 22.1–14

While numerous critics have considered this parable to be an edited duplicate of that found in Luke **14**.16–24, there is no reason at all why our Lord should not have used the same central theme with variations to serve two connected, though different, purposes. The emphasis in the Lukan parable is on the open graciousness of the inviter; in the Matthaean version, it is on the solemn responsibility of the invitee.

Despite a double call (3 f. at least *one* was customary in the Near East at that time), those summoned treated the invitation with disdain (3, 5). While critics have sought to view vs. 6 f. as a later interpolation in the light of the fall of Jerusalem and with allusion to **21**.35 ff., the textual evidence for this is meagre in the extreme. In any case, if the wedding was to be the occasion for the public recognition of the king's son as the royal heir, such action as described in these two verses would have been justified. The invitation to the wedding went on to be offered to others without regard to status or manner of life (9 f.) and such invitees responded with gratifying readiness and in ample numbers (10). Few Jews hearing the parable could have failed to read the message!

However, responsibility does not end with an outward gesture. An appropriate robe was evidently available on request for all guests attending a feast of such importance. In spite of this, one man showed manifest disregard for the high honour of the occasion (11 f.) 'His conduct argued utter insensibility regarding that to which he had been called' (Edersheim). Previous unpreparedness was no excuse for not availing oneself of that which was both necessary and proper and the penalty for such flagrant haughtiness was exclusion from the inner brilliancy of the banqueting hall into 'outer darkness' (13).

True evangelism involves 'persuasion' as well as 'proclamation', not in the sense of pressurizing people into the Kingdom but by urging upon them, with true compassion, God's gracious offer of salvation (cf. Acts 2.40 f.; 24.25 ff.) Those who reject such an offer, especially through such downright indifference as has been illustrated for us in this parable, will be held responsible for their actions. The lines of divine judgement in Scripture are clearly drawn (13 f., cf. Acts 17.31) and one of the greatest tragedies of the contemporary world is a complete unawareness of their reality.

What are some of the modern parallels of the excuses of v. 5 in relation to men's rejection of the gospel today?

26: Men Challenged

John 21.1-19

A wearying night's fishing (1-3) was transformed by a miracle at daybreak (4-8) and concluded with a lakeside breakfast (9-14). This, in its turn, led on to a personal conversation of moving intimacy between our Lord and Peter (15-19). Since the days when he had been led to Jesus (cf. 1.42), Peter had slowly learned the nature of discipleship, but his brave professions of outstanding loyalty (cf. 13.37; Matt. 26.33) had been shattered by the challenges of a serving maid in the Temple courtyard (cf. Matt. 26.69 ff.). Around the embers of the charcoal fire (9), perhaps withdrawn somewhat from the rest of the disciples, Jesus presses upon Peter the basic realities of spiritual relationship and service.

With the well-known variation in choice of words (see a very helpful discussion of this in W. Hendriksen's commentary on John, pp. 494-500), our Lord probes Peter regarding the comparative nature (15), genuineness (16) and basic quality (17) of his love. To each of Peter's responses, our Lord gives a new com-

mission. Peter, once designated to be 'a fisher of men' (cf. Matt.
4.19) is now called to be a shepherd of men too, and with another
gentle movement in the choice of words, Jesus introduces Peter
to his ministry of 'providing food for the little ones of the flock'
(15), 'caring for the sheep' (16) and 'providing food for the sheep'
(17). Jesus had already spoken to His disciples about His own
ministry as Shepherd (10.1–30). Now He was disclosing the
responsibility of those whom God would appoint to be 'under-
shepherds' (cf. Acts 20.28; 1 Pet. 5.2) of His people, that these
might be fed 'with knowledge and understanding' (cf. Jer. 3.15).

Among God's gifts to His Church are 'pastors and teachers to
equip God's people for work in His service' (Eph. 4.11 f., NEB).
The ministry of all such will need Christ's own character and
service as their pattern, together with the example of the errant
shepherds of Israel in Ezekiel's day (Ezek. 34.1 ff.) serving as a
shameful warning against lethargy and irresponsibility.

The Church's mission today needs a more genuine pastoral
care both for those within and without its fellowship. It is
salutary to be reminded that while this must be expressed particularly by the Church's leaders it should also be evident in the
life of each individual Christian (Phil. 2.1 ff.).

*Is Christ calling you to 'follow' Him further in a ministry of
greater caring for people?*

27: Men Commissioned

Matthew 28.16–20; Mark 16.14–20

The whole of our Lord's life was an expression of divine authority
(cf. Matt. 11.27; John 3.35; 13.3; 17.2), from His declared
prerogative to forgive sins (Matt. 9.6) to His complete control over
the disposition of His earthly life (John 10.18). With a retrospec-
tive glance at His victory on the Cross (Col. 2.15) and in anticipation of the final culmination of this victory (Phil. 2.9), Jesus
again affirms that complete sovereignty is His. This sovereignty
had once been subtly but only partially offered to Him by Satan
(Matt. 4.8 f.), but which now 'had been given' (aorist tense,
indicating a past event) to Him by His Father (Matt. 28.18).

Such universal authority forms the basis of the Church's
universal mission (28.19). 'The narrow path within Israel had to

branch out into the wide world of all nations' (Karl Barth), and the disciples were commissioned to bring men to be what they themselves already were, administering baptism 'into' or 'as a sign of their new state of belonging to' (Gk. *eis*) the triune God. Discipleship is no less than an entry into a life of loving obedience to Christ (cf. John 14.15) and His presence is pledged to His ambassadors until 'the consummation of the present age' (28.20).

The words of the 'Great Commission' (Matt. 28.18 f.; Mark 16.15) have figured prominently in the motivating reasons for modern missionary movement. At the outset, they were the main source of appeal for William Carey and have been writ large into our missionary literature and hymnology. However, it is important to see them in their wider Biblical context. True missionary motivation can never consist of mere obedience to an external command; it must essentially spring from the energies of the Holy Spirit whose ministry it is to write the law of God on the heart of each believer (cf. Jer. 31.33; John 16.14 f.), moving him in a spontaneous obedience to God's purposes. This is what lay behind Peter's 'we cannot but speak' (Acts 4.20) and all the spontaneous evangelistic zeal so evident in the Early Church.

Note: Mark 16.9–20 was relegated to the margin by the RSV translators but the genuine place of the passage in the apostolic tradition can still be defended, and indeed in the second edition of the RSV it appears in the main body of the text.

How much is an over-emphasis on 'obedience to the Great Commission' as a motive and justification for mission a sign of spiritual decadence within the Church?

28: Men Responsible

1 Corinthians 3.1–23

The cult of personality among the believers at Corinth (4) was evidence both of their spiritual immaturity (2) and carnality (3). Paul 'levels' first himself, the one who first brought the gospel to Corinth (Acts 18.1 ff.), and then Apollos, one of the 'follow up workers' (Acts 18.27 ff.), with a shattering 'what' (5). He moves the spotlight from the 'idolized' Christian worker to the true 'Worker' who deigns to use human instruments so that men may believe (5). Paul and Apollos performed their work of planting and watering but God was the One who continually (for so the Greek tense indicates) caused spiritual life to grow (6). 'The planter and the waterer are nothing compared with Him who gives life to the seed' (7, J. B. Phillips).

The priority of God in the consideration of the Church's task of mission is further emphasized as Paul sees Christians as being 'junior partners' with God in His work, as well as being spheres of God's creative and constructive activity (9). 'When mission has been defined as essentially a human activity or even as man's obedience to God's command, sooner or later its mainspring has snapped under the pressure of events . . . Fundamentally, mission is not man's action but God's; it is for the Christian to choose whether he will be caught up into it and participate in it, or remain outside' (J. V. Taylor).

The precedence of God in mission brings its own solemn responsibility to those who are His instruments. As 'site building supervisors' (10, Gk. *architectōn*) under divine appointment, the manner and materials of their building work must match the nature of the foundation (10 ff.). It may be easier to go for what is cheap and easily available, but there is a time coming when a man's work will be evaluated for what it truly is (13, the word translated 'revealed' means 'shown up in true character'). The New Testament frequently sets this prospect of the final accounting Day of God before us (e.g. 5.5; 2 Cor. 1.14; 2 Pet. 3.12). While a believer's salvation will not be at stake (15, cf. 1 Cor. 9.27) the lasting worthwhileness of his service will be.

How much is your present service truly 'worth' in terms of eternal values?

29: Men Converted

1 Thessalonians 1

The church in the strategically located, Roman provincial capital of Thessalonica (1) had a quality about it that was outstanding. The presentation of the gospel to them in the first instance was not with the customary parade of words expected from travelling orators (cf. 1 Cor. 1.17; 2.4), but with a spiritual power and an exemplary conduct which commended, not contradicted, the message (5, cf. 2.10). The Holy Spirit once again fulfilled the ministry about which Jesus had formerly spoken (John 16.8 ff.) and enabled the Thessalonians to accept the gospel with joy (cf. Gal. 5.22; Rom. 14.17) in the midst of persecution (6, cf. Acts 17.1 ff.). Theirs was a genuine and lasting turning (9, cf. Acts 14.15) and no superficial 'decision' induced by human persuasion.

Such a 'birth' led to outstanding 'growth'. Faith 'showed itself in action' (NEB), their new love 'toiled' in its practical outworking and their hope exhibited 'not the sort of patience which grimly waits for the end but the patience which radiantly hopes for the dawn' (W. Barclay, cf. vs. 3, 10). Further, their lives took on something of the character of Christ and His messengers (6, cf. 1 Cor. 4.16) and they in their turn began to commend the gospel which had been unmistakably imprinted on their lives (7; Gk. *tupos*, translated 'example', was originally used in relation to the impression of a die). All this could not happen without there being an 'overflow', and so it is not surprising that we read that they had become 'a sort of sounding board' (J. B. Phillips) for their faith. Not only most of Greece (the area covered by the Roman provinces of Macedonia and Achaia) but in a seemingly endless variety of other places (Paul uses the word 'everywhere' in hyperbolic fashion), news of their faith had spread (8). Paul found himself unemployed (8)!

We discern here the pattern of all true evangelism. 'A church in every community and thereby the gospel to every creature' was Paul's strategy. Unless we are prepared to take the nature and nurture of local churches with greater seriousness today, our worldwide evangelistic task will continue to be over-weighted with 'professional' missionary endeavour, and thus lose a vast amount of its momentum. How good it is to hear, for example, of Indian believers witnessing widely among their fellow-countrymen and Brazilian churches sending missionaries to Africa!

How much do you pray and work for 'sounding board' churches overseas?

Questions and themes for study and discussion on Studies 23-29

1. What do Luke 10.10–16; Acts 17.31 and Rom. 2.16 teach on man's responsibility in the hearing of the gospel?

2. 'The integrity of mission can only be accounted for by a theology of love' (Douglas Webster). Do you agree?
3. What are the main New Testament principles regarding the relationship of a missionary to newly planted churches?

FIVE

Paul the Missionary

30: Called by the Spirit

Acts 13.1–12

Paul had received early notice of what his life's mission was to be
(22.15, 21; 26.16 ff.; Gal. 1.16). Barnabas, with his large-hearted
capacity for the work of God, recognized in him a man of God
with considerable spiritual potential, and brought him to Antioch
(11.23–26). Together, they taught the new believers there. Barnabas and Paul were among the gifts Christ had begun to give to the
Antiochan church (1, cf. 1 Cor. 12.28 ff.; Eph. 4.11) and during
the course of one of the leaders' seasons of worship (accompanied
by fasting to encourage greater spiritual earnestness, cf. 14.23)
the Holy Spirit exercised His ministry of selection and direction
for the work of the gospel (2). It is probable that the will of
the Spirit was made known through the utterance of one of the
prophets, who, with his colleagues, expressed the oneness of the
church in the new venture by a further period of waiting on God
and in the laving on of hands (3, cf. 6.6). In this way, they were
'let go' by the church and 'sent out' by the Spirit (3 f.). 'The world
ministry which thus began was destined to change the history of
Europe and the world' (E.M. Blaiklock).

There are a number of ways in the New Testament in which
God through His Spirit disperses His servants in order to spread
the gospel. Sometimes, He uses the uncomfortable events of
persecution (8.1, 4; 11.19 f.); at other times, individual guidance,
apparently unrelated to fellow Christians (8.5, 26, 39 f.). But when
it comes to someone closely linked in service with a local church
fellowship, He ensures that the church itself is not only aware of
what He is doing but is linked in full sympathy (cf. 16.1 ff.). There
are times when it is right for individual Christians not to 'confer
with flesh and blood' (Gal. 1.16) in finding God's will; but what
a tragedy when this becomes the practice of young people in
local churches interested in missionary service!

Paul's first recorded encounter as a missionary with paganism

41

bore the characteristics of much that was to follow: forthright proclamation of the evangel (5), interest and response (7, 12) and full-faced opposition (8 f.). The pattern has not changed over the centuries!

What does your church know of the voice of the Spirit in relation to the service of its members (2)?

31: Emboldened with the Word

Acts 13.42–14.7

The three major features of Paul's ministry which emerged at the end of the last study are seen more clearly in today's section. We see firstly the *forthright proclamation* of the divine message, called variously 'the word of God' (13.44, 46, 48, 49), 'the word of His (God's) grace' (14.3) or simply 'the gospel' (14.7). The 'subjects' (13.42, NEB) on which Paul spoke were the mighty accounts of God's deeds in Israel's history (13.16–41) in which the God of Abraham, Moses and David was clearly identified with the God and Father of Jesus Christ who now offered men forgiveness of sins (13.38), and eternal life, 'the life of the age to come' (13.46, 48), an age which in Christ had now dawned. The very certainty of the message conditioned the manner of presenting it (cf. the 'boldly' of 13.46; 14.3). Neither hint of apology nor quiver of fear do we discern. These were men under commission (1 Cor. 9.17), ambassadors for the living Christ (2 Cor. 5.20), and were wholly taken up with their task.

In the second place, we notice the *fierce opposition* that such preaching aroused. This came initially from the Jews (13.45) and then, at the instigation of the latter, among various sections of the community at large (13.50; 14.2, 5). It took on a variety of forms ranging from open contradiction and the reviling of the message (13.45) to a poisoning of personal attitudes (14.2) and hostile acts of rejection (13.50; 14.5). The Jews not only reacted against the actual message but were no doubt thoroughly aggrieved at the way Paul so easily drew away the 'Gentile worshippers' (13.43, NEB). Once more, however, we notice how God makes the wrath of man to praise Him through causing persecution against His people to become a means for the wider spread of the gospel (14.6 f., cf. 8.4; 11.19).

The third leading characteristic of the witness both of Paul and the Early Church was the *fruitful consequences* evident in the conversion of men and women. In contrast to the blatant opposition of the Jews was the eager responsiveness of the Gentiles to whom he subsequently turned (13.42, 44, 48), and the fulfilment of Isaiah's prediction regarding the world-wide ministry of Christ (13.47; Isa. 49.6) was marked by that abundant joy already noted wherever men have received the gospel (13.48, 52, cf. 1 Thess. 1.6).

Is part of the reason why we do not see more of features two and three today found in our weakness on feature one?

32: Caring for the Churches

Acts 15.36–16.10

The relatedness of all of Paul's ministry to the founding and nurturing of local churches is nowhere more evident than in this passage. His 'Come, let us return . . .' (36) was spoken in full remembrance of the fierce treatment he had previously received in those same regions of Asia (e.g. 14.5, 19). His ministry of 'bringing new strength to the congregations' (15.41, 16.5, NEB) was effected in two ways: through his personal ministry of teaching, and his presentation of the guidelines drawn up by the apostles and elders at Jerusalem (15.23; 16.4). It was typical of what was to follow throughout his life, not only during his subsequent missionary journeys (e.g. 20.2, 17 ff.), but also through the medium of his writings, which were basically not evangelistic documents but Bible teaching 'letters to young churches' (J. B. Phillips). Much of the work of overseas missionaries today is involved with just such a 'nurturing ministry' among younger churches. The strategic work of those engaged in such spheres as Bible College teaching or lay leadership training must be viewed every way as important as that of the more 'traditional' jungle pioneer or rural doctor.

To fulfil his task of preaching and teaching, Paul needed colleagues. He himself had once been chosen by Barnabas (11.25) and had soon become the senior partner (note the change from 'Barnabas and Saul' in 11.30; 12.25, etc., to 'Paul and Barnabas' from 13.43 onwards). Now came *his* turn to select, and the first

43

occasion was not an entirely happy affair (15.37 ff.). Paul's personal judgement (cf. 38, NEB) led to 'a sharp clash of opinion' (39, J. B. Phillips) which led to 'a parting asunder', 'an uncommonly strong expression (E. M. Blaiklock). Unlike Barnabas, Paul was not prepared to wait for men to develop into greater maturity but looked for more 'instant' reliability and effectiveness. Paul had no doubt taken note of Silas' character both during the journey from Jerusalem to Antioch and during Silas' ministry there (15.22, 32), and chose him accordingly.

In the event, the division between Paul and Barnabas resulted in a wider spread of the gospel (15.39–41), and it is good to read of Paul's subsequent esteem of Mark's usefulness in Christian service (2 Tim. 4.11). Paul's selection of Timothy (16.1 ff.) was much more straightforward, particularly as the young man was commended by the Lystran church (cf. 1 Tim. 1.18; 4.14). Thus, continually directed by the Spirit (16.6 ff.), Paul moved on with his colleagues in glad obedience to the unfolding pattern of God's call to him (16.10), carrying his 'daily . . . responsibility for all the churches' (2 Cor. 11.28; J. B. Phillips).

Do you 'care' enough for young believers?

33: Preaching to the Greeks

Acts 17.16–34

When Paul arrived at Athens, he could remain no mere onlooker when confronted with the hundreds of temples and pagan sculptures that 'filled' the city (16). What he saw with his eyes made a sharp, spiritual impact within him (16), and this in turn prompted him to positive action (17 f.), a very commendable sequence indeed!

He was met with a level of opposition and unbelief that he had rarely encountered in his previous ministry: the 'professional philosophers' of the Athenian debating circle who wished to pick the brains of this supposed 'cock sparrow' of an orator (18, J. B. Phillips). The amazing ability and versatility of Paul's trained mind (cf. 22.3) are seen very clearly in what proved to be 'Paul's first major exposition of the gospel to an audience without a background of Old Testament theology or Jewish thought' (E. M. Blaiklock).

It is important to see that Paul did not set out in the first place to identify their 'unknown deity' with the one, true God he knew (23). Rather, he declared his intention of announcing to them the truth about God in view of the fact that they had, in this open way, confessed their ignorance about it. Paul went on to affirm some of the great truths about God, His creatorship (24), His self-sufficiency (25), His sovereignty over, and design for, man, all planned so that man himself should respond to Him in worship (26 f.). In relation to this theme Paul goes on to quote two extracts from Stoic poetry dealing with the Greeks' devotion for Zeus, 'considered . . . the Supreme Being of Greek philosophy' (F. F. Bruce), readily acknowledging that even in the midst of pagan thought, there are some glimpses of truth to be found. As he moves to the major thrust of his sermon, however, Paul makes the issue abundantly clear. Man must put aside all his pretensions and projections about ultimate reality and the sort of 'god' he imagines to be 'there', and repent and believe in the risen Son of God, the Judge of all (30 f.).

No worship, outside the Hebrew-Christian tradition of God's revelation as contained in the Old and New Testaments, can possibly be truly satisfying to man or acceptable with God, however sincere it may be. Man may grope and grasp for God, but because of the devastation within him caused by sin (Rom. 3.9 ff.) he can never truly find Him. *Only in Jesus Christ is the true meeting point to be found, and in all* dialogue and encounter with men of other faiths, this must be the centre of the Christian's message, even as it was Paul's.

'Paul was not a man to take a complete holiday from the main business of his life' (F. F. Bruce). How often do you?

34: Engaging in the Conflict

2 Corinthians 10

Relationships between Christian workers and those among whom they minister are of major importance in the work of God, and Paul undoubtedly had his full complement of problems in this realm! Some of the believers at Corinth accused him of a divided approach (1) and worldly motives (2) and, consequently, of a lack of authority to teach them (8). In the midst of misunderstandings and suspicions like these, Paul realized that only an approach modelled on that of his Lord would prove adequate (1). On the one hand there must be 'gentleness' (NEB, the Greek word means basically 'strength under control' cf. Matt. 11.29) and 'magnanimity' (NEB, the Greek word signifies the exercise of justice tempered with love and understanding as well as exactness cf. John 8.1–11). On the other hand there must be a blend of firmness and consistency (2, 11, cf. Matt. 21.12 ff.; 23.13 ff.). This is always the right way forward for Christian workers involved in similar situations.

Together with these 'internal battles', Paul was faced with the major 'external' battle against the entrenched strongholds of evil in the hearts of men (4 f.). He knew that behind the 'sophistries' (5, NEB) and 'every towering obstacle erected to prevent men from knowing God' (W. Barclay) was the activity of the Evil One whose purpose and work it was both to blind and bind men in unbelief (cf. 2 Cor. 4.4; 2 Tim. 2.26). He realized that such activity could only be confronted and defeated by spiritual means (4, cf. Psa. 20.7; Eph. 6.12 ff.), a truth that Christians today need to bear firmly in mind. With so much importance at the present time being placed in human organization, prowess and resources, whenever the Church forgets the essentially spiritual nature of the battle in which she is engaged, impotence and defeat come upon her immediately.

In the midst of such battles, Paul knew himself to be a man under divine direction, with limits of service clearly demarcated for him (13). He realized that God was the great Commander of operations for the advance of His Kingdom among men, and if all His servants were obedient to Him, there would be no overlapping (14 f.). The challenge of the 'lands beyond' (16) was ever on his heart (cf. Rom. 15.20). He knew, however, that to venture further afield without properly fulfilling the initial task God had given him, i.e. the building up of the faith of the newly born church (8, 15), was to court the superficial.

Obedience to the Divine Commander leads both to victory and effectiveness in Christian service. How obedient are you?

35: Protesting for the Truth

2 Corinthians 11

Paul was the founder of the Corinthian church (1 Cor. 4.15; 2 Cor. 10.14) and consequently felt a particular burden of responsibility for its healthy development and doctrinal purity. He was continually aware of the dangers of invading viruses and parasitic growths that would damage the church's well-being (cf. Acts 20.29 ff.; Phil. 3.2), and he was faced with this very danger at Corinth through the activities of 'sham-apostles' (13, NEB) who were preaching 'a different gospel' (4, Gal. 1. 6ff.) and masquerading under the guise of being true teachers of God's Word (14 f.; Matt. 7.15). Such men were 'courting' those whose love was intended to be 'single hearted' for Christ, and in doing so were the very instruments of Satan (2 f.).

While having no desire to parade his own credentials, Paul knew that the growth of the young church and the truth of the gospel were at stake. Thus, he urges the Corinthian believers to consider two main aspects of his ministry. Firstly, the sources of his financial support (7–11) surely indicated to them that he was not out for mercenary gain. He had a right to 'earn his living by the gospel', being supported by the free-will offerings of those to whom he ministered (cf. 1 Cor. 9. 3–18); yet at Corinth he had been supported initially through his own tent-making work (Acts 18.1 ff.) and later by gifts from other churches (8 f.). This was the only 'robbery' he had committed among them (8)! In the second place, there were the incontrovertible marks of the manner of man that he was and what preaching the gospel had meant for him in terms of suffering and risk to life itself (22–33). His Hebrew upbringing (cf. Phil. 3.5), the extent and hazards of his evangelistic ministries and finally, in contrast to these 'external things' (28, NEB), the inward burden of love he carried for the young congregations which demanded unreserved and sympathetic self-giving in all situations (28 f.), were surely sufficient evidences of the genuineness of his ministry. Paul called God Himself to witness to the veracity of such details (31). 'There has been no inaccuracy and no over-statement' (R. V. G. Tasker).

For world mission, mastery of the language, adoption of new customs, and exertion of abundant energy are all needed; but a man's or woman's ministry stands or falls in the end by the quality of their life.

47

In the long term, no 'outward show' can hide the true nature of inward quality. How genuine is your service?

36: Captured by the Gospel
Philippians 1.1–18

The outflow of Paul's life for the progress of the gospel (12) stamps these verses. Paul writes to a church that he had been instrumental in founding (Acts 16.12 ff.) and nourishing (Acts 20.1 ff.), and which had developed sufficiently both to appoint its own leadership (1) and to partner him in the work of the gospel (5). His dominant concern is for their continuing growth in life and character, in a love that was not blind but 'full of knowledge and wise insight' (9, J. B. Phillips). He longed that they might both aim for and attain the highest in holy living (10), showing the evidences of the presence of the risen Christ within them (11, cf. John 15.4 ff.; Col. 1.10). 'His heart throbbed with the heart of Christ' (J. B. Lightfoot, 8) in a pulsation that was expressed through the twin channels of Christian instruction and prayer (4, 9, cf. Col. 1.9 ff., etc.). That Paul could in this way maintain his ministry to those from whom he was separated is inescapable evidence of the supreme quality of his own love and care for them (cf. 4.1, etc.).

Were he to have been in the quiet of a 'missionary residence' at the time, such warm, earnest writing would have been quite understandable. But he was held in a Roman prison (12), chained to the leg of one of his captors (13, the word 'praetorian' could indicate the emperor's palace in Rome or the headquarters of a district governor). In such circumstances, love could not be bound, and neither could the gospel itself, as Paul himself gladly goes on to testify (12–14). This was not the only time when Paul had cause to glory in the 'unchainable' gospel (cf. 2 Tim. 2.9) and even though the preaching of it was undertaken at times with mixed motives (15–18) as long as 'Christ is set forth' (18, NEB), there could be few grounds for despondency.

The gospel can break out of every circumstance, and the measure to which it does so is a measure of the Christian's spiritual maturity and effectiveness in service.

'In prison . . . Paul was as much on duty as the guards who were posted to watch over him' (R. P. Martin).

37: Setting out the Standard

1 Thessalonians 2.1-16

As Paul reflects on the abundant worthwhileness of his visit to Thessalonica (1), some of the leading characteristics of his apostolic ministry shine forth. In all that he suffered (Acts 16.19-24), Paul exhibited a divinely given *courage* that caused him to declare the gospel 'frankly and fearlessly' (2, NEB). In contrast to the activities of the wandering street orators of the day, his preaching was with *integrity*, devoid of deceitful or debased motives (3, 5). His presentation of the evangel centred in a thoroughgoing sense of *responsibility* in relation to the 'gospel of God' (the phrase occurs three times in vs. 2, 8, and 9 and by inference in v. 4) with which he had been entrusted (cf. Gal. 2.7; 1 Tim. 1.11). In a spirit of *selflessness* (6), he held back from insisting on proper standing and rights as an envoy of Christ (cf. 1 Cor. 9.4 ff.; 2 Thess. 3.9) but gave himself as a father to his children in a *compassion* that expressed itself in gentleness (7) and carried the individual with it (8, Gk. *psuchē* 'selves' denotes here the whole personality rather than 'a body-entombed soul', a concept quite alien to the Scriptures). 'It is still true that vital Christian service is costly' writes Leon Morris. Not for Paul a path of ease, whether this implied the laborious toil (a strong Gk. word) and fatigue (9) of *hard work* or an uncompromising life of *godliness* (10; the three words Paul used in relation to his holy living stress religious devotion, legal rectitude and moral purity respectively, cf. 1.5 f.). Only such a quality of life could commend the *care* he showed for the believers' spiritual development (11 f.).

Let no one underestimate the demands made on those who are called to minister in the name of Christ whether it be among men of a similar or dissimilar culture. Only Christ can give the strength sufficient 'for these things' (2 Cor. 3.5 f.).

How much does your life show the above seven characteristics?

38: Building up the Faith

1 Thessalonians 2.17-3.13

To proclaim the gospel is one thing; to see this gospel being

49

clothed effectively with renewed humanity is another. It was the latter desire that constituted Paul's longing to be assured of the Thessalonian believers' spiritual health and growth. He is concerned primarily about the stability of their 'faith', a word mentioned no less than 5 times in this passage. This was an obvious focus for Satan's attacks (3, 5) just as his own movements were proving to be at that time (2.18; cf. Acts 17.8; 18.6, 12). These young believers were the fruit of his missionary activity, the joyous and glorious evidences that he had not served his Lord in vain (2.19 f.); and news of their firm stand in the gospel made all the difference to his daily living (8 f.).

If Paul 'feared' for them (3.5), it was because he realized the danger of their becoming discouraged by the opposition they were encountering on account of their Christian profession. It was not that he had not warned them of the inevitability of such (4, cf. Matt. 5.11 f., Acts 14.22; 1 Pet. 4.12 f.) but real-life encounters always bring their own unique challenge however much careful preparation there has been beforehand. In any event, suffering for Christ was seen to be an essential accompaniment of following Him. 'What had been an acute problem to faith in Old Testament times—the suffering of the righteous—had come to be recognized as an essential element in God's purposes for His people' (*New Bible Commentary*).

The chief means of nourishment for faith in such circumstances is a ministry of establishing and exhortation (the latter verb is the one derived from the word 'Counseller' or 'Comforter' in John 14.16, 26, etc. cf. Study 16), and the one who was sent to fulfil it (3.2) returned with the glad news of the fruit of it (3.6). With the bright expectation and implication of the return of Christ particularly in view (2.19; 3.13), Paul prayerfully anticipates the Thessalonians' further progress in love and holiness (12 f.) through the direct ministry of the Lord Himself and, eventually, he trusts, through himself (11).

Wise parental care and an adequate, balanced diet are essential prerequisites through a child's early years if strong effective adulthood is to be realized. This is as true in the work of God among men as it is in the child-care centre!

Have you a 'Timothean ministry' (3.2) to fulfil with someone or some church?

Questions and themes for study and discussion on Studies 30-38

1. 'In all the four instances, then, of sending out Barnabas, Saul, Silas and Timothy, what the New Testament emphasizes is *not* the initiative of the individual ... but always the initiative of others ...' (Michael Griffiths). What practical application does this have to missionary recruitment today?

2. 'Many of us today are intellectually embarrassed to speak of the lostness of the lost' (Francis Schaeffer). Why is this so?

3. How can the strategic nature of caring for growing and developing overseas churches be better understood and appreciated when the work of the 'jungle pioneer' continues to make such strong traditional appeal in local churches today?

SIX

Motive for Mission

39: Sharing Good News

2 Kings 6.24–7.20

The four lepers (7.3) were faced with an agonizingly difficult choice. Conditions inside the beleaguered city of Samaria had reached starvation level (6.25) even to the point of cannibalism (6.28). To stay in the 'no man's land' situation at the city gates was equally hopeless. The only prospect of survival was in a show of mercy on the part of the hostile Syrians (7.4), not a very bright possibility. However, they followed this gleam of hope (7.5), leaving the forlorn Israelites shut up to despair behind them, and entered into an unbelievable experience of deliverance and abundance (7.7 f.). The contrast between the city gate and the Syrian camp could hardly have been more amazing!

In the midst of their immeasurable enjoyment, they suddenly realized the responsibility that was theirs in relation to those who were as equally needy as themselves yet still unaware that such bounty was available (7.9). A sense of shame and guilt overtook them as the essentially selfish nature of their actions broke upon them. Inaction and delay were put aside, and with a 'come, let us go and tell . . .' they moved off to share the 'good news' of their discovery with others.

The joy of personal experience and the inescapable sense of obligation to share the reason for it with others blend to form a dominant motive for Christian witness. The believer testifies to that which he had 'heard . . . seen . . . looked on and touched' (1 John 1.1), a principle that finds a practical outworking in numerous New Testament situations (e.g. John 1.40–46; 4.28 ff.; 20.18 ff.). This desire to witness should be irrepressible (Acts 4.20) even amidst opposition (Acts 5.41; 8.4).

Of course, people take some convincing at times! The inhabitants of Samaria were full of incredulity at first when they heard of the miraculous deliverance that God had provided for them (7.12 ff.). 'It's too good to be true!' is the often repeated remark (cf. John 20.25) when the Christian tells of God's wonderful grace revealed in Jesus Christ. But the evidence is there to be investigated and verified (7.15) and, in the last resort, men and women have only themselves to blame if they wish to remain imprisoned in a city where death is the only prospect (John 3.36).

Does the injunction of 1 Pet. 3.15 find you basically lazy?

40: Indebted to Men

Romans 1.1–17

Paul knew that his ministry as an apostle of Christ and as a spokesman for the gospel was not the result of a personal choice but of a divine commissioning (1, cf. 1 Cor. 1.1; 9.17). The scope of this mandate embraced men and women of 'all nations' (5) and he thus found himself under a sense of obligation in preaching the gospel to them (14). Among the Gentiles his potential hearers were of very mixed quality indeed. On the one hand, there were the educated and civilized Greeks, whom many regarded as having no need of further enlightenment; on the other, there were the ignorant and rough-hewn Barbarians who were usually set aside as completely beyond the bounds of any moral improvement. But Paul knew that both groups stood in equal need because of their common 'sinnership' before God (Rom. 3.19, 23). He knew that it was only through the gospel that the power of God was available for the overthrow of evil and the establishing of righteousness in the hearts of men whoever they were and wherever they were to be found (16 f.). 'Paul was their debtor not by any right that either Greeks or Barbarians had acquired over him but by the destination which God had given to his ministry towards them' (R. Haldane).

Of course, this gospel which had God as its author (1) and Christ as its focus (3, 9) met with widespread rejection wherever it was proclaimed. The Jews met it with hostility because of its claim to supersede the Law and to identify Jesus as Messiah. The Gentiles met it with contempt because to vaunt death on a cross as a triumph of any sort was deemed to be plain stupidity (1 Cor. 1.23). Despite all this, Paul was proud to testify to the power of the gospel in his own life and to tell it forth unashamedly

(16). He gloried in the Cross (Gal. 6.14), and the desire to make its message known among men impelled him ever forward (15, cf. 2 Cor. 10.16).

How up to date are you in the repayment of your spiritual debts to your fellow men?

41: Proclaiming Salvation

Romans 10

In spite of all that he had suffered for the gospel's sake from his fellow-countrymen, Paul's practical and prayerful concern for their salvation was irresistible (1). It sprang from his firm understanding of the uniqueness of God's work of grace in reckoning men guiltless before Him on the grounds of the death and resurrection of Jesus Christ mediated to them by their act of personal faith (4, 9 f.). No human grouping had preferential treatment from the One who was ready to give His grace in abundant measure to all who called on Him (12 f.). No major exertion was needed to bring this salvation within reachable distance (6 f.); 'Christ is ever available to faith and so likewise is the gospel' (*New Bible Commentary*). It grieved Paul that the Jews, of all people, could display such 'unenlightened zeal' in expending their energies on a way of living that could never bring them into a right relationship with God (2 ff.).

From the major principle of 'salvation in Christ alone', there arose the major corollary that men had to hear the good news first of all in order to have an opportunity to believe it, and for them to hear it, messengers were needed to proclaim it (14). This commitment of God to human instrumentality is both awesome and yet eminently reasonable. The gospel contains spiritual truths presented in an ordered and intelligible manner. In order to receive the benefits Christ waits to bestow, men must know who He is, what He has done for men and what they, in turn, must do to receive His salvation. What better way to hear than through those who have come to know these truths in their own personal experience? Certainly, the possibility of believing in an 'incognito Christ' or finding Christ as Saviour through sincere religious questionings within a non-Christian religious system such as Hinduism or Buddhism, while attractive speculation, hardly squares with the nature of the gospel or the nature of man as a rational, responsible being.

If men can only be saved through response to the Christian gospel, then it must, with all speed, be taken to them by human messengers and it is apparent that this urgency was one that gripped Paul throughout his missionary activity. Certainly, his feet moved swiftly to 'preach the good news' (15, Isa. 52.7) even if those who were best prepared to receive it proved uninterested and unresponsive (18, 21). The responsibility of 'the watchman' is basically unaffected by the response of those to whom he declares his warning (Ezek. 33.1 ff.). His part is to 'blow the trumpet' and 'warn the people'; theirs is to 'turn and live' or face the inevitable alternative.

How much urgency is there in your Christian witness?

42: Stewarding Responsibly

1 Corinthians 9.13–27

Few other passages in the New Testament reveal so much of Paul's motivation in mission as this one. He declares first of all that although he had every right, as a minister of the gospel to be supported by the voluntary offerings of those who benefited from his teaching (13 f.), yet he preferred to preach 'without expense to anyone' (18, NEB). His motivation lay not in the expectation of sizeable financial reward from a job for which he had personally opted (17), but in response to an inner compulsion which 'bore in' upon him (16; note the use of the verb 'to lay' in such verses as Luke 5.1 where it is translated 'pressed' and Acts 27.20). He was a man under divine appointment (cf. Study 40), committed to a task of responsible 'stewardship' (the root meaning of the word 'commission', 17). In the Graeco-Roman world, a steward was a person called to a right use of that which had been entrusted to him by another (1 Cor. 4.1 f.) and for Paul this meant the effective sharing of the grace of God with men (Eph. 3.2, 7 f.). This responsibility lay in two directions: towards God, whom he served and whose gospel he proclaimed (1 Tim. 1.11), and towards men, who stood in such need of this gospel and to whom he had been sent (Acts 26.17). Individual patterns of involvement will vary, but such stewardship is held by every

Christian, for it arises out of the very nature of the gospel itself.

The message of God's grace so gripped Paul that in order to win men for Jesus Christ, he was ready to go to any lengths necessary within the bounds of his Christian commitment (19 ff.) and without compromising the gospel itself (cf. Gal. 2.11 ff.). He likened his manner of living to that of an athlete who needed to maintain optimum physical fitness and single-heartedness of purpose for the event for which he was entered (24 ff.). The race was there to be won and the opponent in the ring there to be hit (26)! If such purpose and concentration could characterize the sportsman, Paul reasoned, how much more should the Christian bruise his own body and 'make it know its master' (27, NEB) to serve his Lord acceptably. With the context of the whole passage being 'service' rather than 'salvation', Paul's fear was not that he might finally be lost—he knew that for him, as for all true believers, this was impossible (Rom. 8.29 f., 38; Phil. 1.6, etc.)— but that if he neglected his own 'spiritual fitness', God might have to set him aside in preference for others who were more usable.

How 'spiritually fit' are you for Christ's service (1 Tim. 4.7)?

43: By Love Constrained

2 Corinthians 5.10–21

The knowledge that he was answerable to a divine tribunal (10) produced in Paul a humble and obedient reverence before God (11). This, in its turn, led to a purposeful attitude to others as he 'addressed his appeal' (cf. NEB) to them regarding the gospel by which they also one day would be judged (Rom. 2.16; 1 Cor. 4.5). A purely dispassionate approach to men with the gospel, embodying 'a take it or leave it' attitude, is quite alien to the pursuance of Christian mission. 'Proclamation' inevitably involves 'persuasion' (cf. Acts 18.4; 28.23) in that person to person encounter in which God Himself is the major Spokesman (20).

Whatever interpretations were put on his ministry (13), Paul knew that his inner motivation was the love of Christ (14). It left him 'no choice' (NEB) and we see the force of the Greek verb in such verses as Luke 8.45, 12.50, and Acts 18.5. The love that moved Christ to have compassion on the multitudes (Matt. 9.36–38) and to touch and heal the leper (Mark 1.41) moved in

Paul's life and moves today in the lives of all who would serve Him, unerringly channelling their actions to others.

Paul had reflected much on this love and had reached firm conclusions (14, NEB). He saw that it embraced 'all'; that 'innumerable company of those who would enjoy the benefits of redemption' (R. V. G. Tasker). He knew that it resulted in newness of life (17, Rom. 6.4) and a restored relationship with God (18 f., Rom. 5.1, 10). Genuine compassion is always grounded in truth and the more this truth is understood, the wider will be the personal experience of the love of God. In this passage, we see a very clear blending of experience and theology, which both shows the dependence of the former on the latter and the inevitable connection between the two. When we try to divorce them, mission becomes distorted and troubles begin to multiply!

How far have you begun to plumb the dimensions of the love of Christ (Eph. 3.18 f.)?

44: Completing the Course

Acts 20.17–38

A race is entered to be finished and won despite all the obstacles and dangers that may be encountered while running it. This was the imagery in which Paul saw the ministry he had 'received from the Lord Jesus' (24). He knew himself to be a man under divine commission (1 Tim. 1.1, 12) and the passion to bear testimony to God's grace dominated his life (24). To effect this ministry with the required humility (19) and perseverance (31) had involved him in a rigorous sequence of suffering (19, 23), hard physical effort for the support of others and himself (34) and a self-giving that cost him emotionally (31) as well as in every other way. Even life itself was held lightly in comparison to the completion of his task (24, cf. Phil. 1.20; 2.17). Through it all, there was a resolute teaching of the Word of God in which he did not flinch from presenting any part of God's truth that, while initially appearing unsavoury to the hearers, was needful for Christian venture (20, 27). Nor did he withhold those centralities of the gospel which, though frequently despised by men, comprised the essential steps to salvation (21, cf. Acts 17.30; 2 Pet. 3.9).

The ministry of Christ was characterized by a similar perseverance that refused to be dimmed or diverted by seemingly more attractive alternatives (Matt. 4.8–10; Luke 9.51; Heb. 12.2) and embodied that tenacity of purpose that had already been prefigured in the person of the Servant of the Lord (Isa. 42.4. See Study 6). Such was the quality that stamped Paul's life and made him righteously yet compassionately indignant about those who had been deluded into surrendering a once firmly held strong intent to follow Christ (Gal. 5.7; 2 Tim. 4.10, cf. Matt. 19.20 ff.).

The men and women who have made their lives count for God are those who have pressed forward with singleness of purpose despite discouragements and temptations to give up. After the disastrous fire in Calcutta in March, 1812, that destroyed many of Carey's manuscripts and large stocks of paper, he could write: 'I wish to be still and know that the Lord is God . . . He will no doubt bring good out of this evil.' 100 years later, C. T. Studd, chided at leaving his home and family at the age of 52 to preach Christ in Africa, replied, 'If Jesus Christ be God and died for me, then no sacrifice can be too great for me to make for Him.' Of such fibre are men of mission made.

Have you learned how to endure with patience and joy (Col. 1.11)?

45: Anticipating the Finale

Revelation 5.1–14; 7.9–17

'The Revelation' is a book of anticipated glory, and an integral part of this glory is the culmination of God's redeeming purposes in the perfecting of His Church. Throughout history, God has been choosing a people to bear His Name among the world's peoples (Acts 15.14, NEB). It is His purpose that this great company should, as part of the riches of its salvation, share in a fellowship of mutual love and service which, while only imperfectly realized during life on earth, will be perfectly attained thereafter. Through the acclamation of the enthroned Lamb, firstly by the four living creatures and the twenty-four elders (5.8) and then by a vast concourse gathered before that heavenly Throne (7.9), John is given a vision of the redeemed of all ages drawn from all segments of human settlement on earth. This multitudinous throng is seen clad in white robes (9), 'perfect in the righteousness of Christ' (L. Morris), and destined to share in a triumphal rule (5.10). Exegetes may wish to identify the two groups of chapters 5 and 7 in different ways, according to which school of biblical interpretation they support, but the above noted characteristics are certainly common to all God's glorified people in every age.

No turn of history or assault of evil can sway God's purposes for the perfecting of His Church (Matt. 16.18; Rom. 8.28–30), and the end of the world will only be ushered in when the last of God's people is brought to a saving knowledge of Himself through faith in His Son. To some, this may appear to paralyse missionary effort; for if this is God's irrevocable purpose, then will He not accomplish it regardless of the obedience of His people? The contrary, however, is the case. 'Instead of rendering evangelism superfluous, election demands evangelism. All of God's elect must be saved. Not one of them may perish. And the gospel is the means by which God bestows saving faith upon them. In fact, it is the only means which God employs to that end.' (R. B. Kuiper).

In the knowledge that Christ's Church is being built among 'all nations', then, the servants of God can set their faces to their world-wide task with much expectation, awaiting both their Master's return (Luke 12.36) and the perfection of the Church in which, by God's grace alone, they themselves will share (Luke 10.20).

Does the biblical doctrine of the Church breed complacency or concern in your life?

Questions and themes for study and discussion on Studies 39–45

1. 'Our supreme need is not a new strategy of mission but a new inspiration for mission' (Douglas Webster). How accurate an analysis is this?
2. What is involved today in being 'put in trust with the gospel' (cf. 1 Thess. 2.3 f.; 1 Tim. 1.11; Titus 1.3)?
3. Illustrate from Scripture and contemporary life the main reason for lack of adequate perseverance in Christian service.

59